Watery Worlds

THE
DEEPEST SEA

Jinny Johnson

W
FRANKLIN WATTS
LONDON • SYDNEY

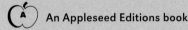 An Appleseed Editions book

Paperback edition 2015

First published in 2011 by Franklin Watts
338 Euston Road, London NW1 3BH

Franklin Watts Australia
Hachette Children's Books
Level 17/207 Kent St, Sydney, NSW 2000

© 2011 Appleseed Editions

Created by Appleseed Editions Ltd,
Well House, Friars Hill, Guestling,
East Sussex TN35 4ET

Designed by Hel James
Illustrations by Graham Rosewarne
Edited by Mary-Jane Wilkins
Picture research by Su Alexander

ISBN 978 1 4451 3828 2
Dewey Classification 577.7'9

A CIP catalogue for this book is available from the British Library.

Picture credits
Title page & contents page Phase4Photography/Shutterstock; 4 Oxford Scientific/
Photolibrary; 5 Bettmann/Corbis; 6 Marevision//Photolibrary; 7t Oceans-Image/
Photoshot/NHPA, b Kevin Raskoff; 8 David Shale/Nature Picture Library; 9 Doc White/
Nature Picture Library; 10 Paulo de Oliveira/Photolibrary; 11 Oxford Scientific/
Photolibrary; 12 Peter Batson/DeepSeaPhotography.com; 13t Karen Gowlett-Holmes/
Photolibrary, b Peter Batson/DeepSeaPhotography.com; 14 Dante Fenolio/Science
Photo Library; 15 Mark Conlin/Photolibrary; 16-17 background Argus/Shutterstock,
16 Jonathan Bird/Photolibrary; 17 Franco Banfi/Photolibrary; 18-19 background
Phase4Photography/Shutterstock, 18 Jonathan Bird/Photolibrary; 19 Bob Cranston/
Photolibrary; 20 The Natural History Museum/Alamy; 21 Florian Graner/Nature Picture
Library; 22 Clive Bromhall/Photolibrary; 23 Doc White/Nature Picture Library;
24 Oceans-Image/Photoshot/NHPA; 25t Bruce Rasner/Rotman/Nature Picture Library,
b Kelvin Aitken/Photolibrary; 26 Scripps Institute Oceanography/Photolibrary;
27t Ralph White/Corbis, b Dr Ken Macdonald/Science Photo Library; 29 Lebrecht
Music and Arts Picture Library/Corbis; 30-31 & 32 Shutterstock
Front cover Mark Conlin/Photolibrary, below left to right:Marevision/Photolibrary,
Peter Batson/DeepSeaPhotography.com, Dante Fenolio/SPL

Printed in China

Franklin Watts is a division of Hachette Children's Books,
an Hachette UK company.
www.hachette.co.uk

Contents

Down in the deep sea

Light from the sun reaches only into the surface waters of the ocean. This layer of the sea is called the **sunlit zone** and it goes down to about 200 metres. Tiny floating plants can live here, so there is plenty of food for plant-eating sea creatures. Larger animals eat the plant-eaters.

This anglerfish, like many deep-sea fish, has a big gaping mouth and long teeth.

Amazing!

The average depth of the ocean is almost four kilometres.

Below the sunlit zone is the **twilight zone**, where there is a small amount of light. Then comes the darkest, deepest sea. There is no light at all in the water below 1,000 metres and the amazing creatures here live in total darkness. We know less about this area of the ocean than any other place on Earth.

Guess what?

The deepest part of the sea is a place called Challenger Deep in the Mariana Trench in the Pacific. It is about 11,000 metres deep and only one manned craft has ever been down there. This was a deep-diving vessel called *Trieste* in 1960 and it had a two-man crew.

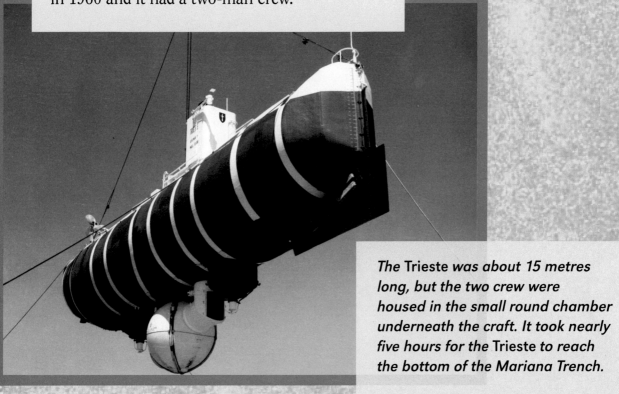

The Trieste *was about 15 metres long, but the two crew were housed in the small round chamber underneath the craft. It took nearly five hours for the* Trieste *to reach the bottom of the Mariana Trench.*

The twilight zone

The twilight zone of the sea is between 200 metres and 1,000 metres down. Here there is some light from above, but not enough light for plants to live.

Some animals swim up to the sunlit waters above to find food every day. Others eat each other or anything that drifts down from the surface. Many fish that live in the twilight zone have very large eyes to help them see, even though there is very little light. The alfonsino fish and the hatchetfish are two of them.

The comb jelly has rows of luminous hairs along its body. These beat to move it through the water.

Guess what?
The barreleye fish has large tube-shaped eyes. These are protected by a transparent cover over the fish's head. The fish can move these amazing eyes upwards to look for **prey**, or forwards if it needs to.

Some kinds of squid, jellyfish and comb jellies are **transparent** (see-through), making it very hard for **predators** to see them.

The bloodbelly comb jelly is a glowing red colour, but in the darkness of the deep sea it appears black and is almost invisible.

Amazing!

Big mouths

Not many creatures live in the deep sea, so food can be hard to find. Many deep-sea fish have extra-large mouths and they swallow almost anything they come across.

The grenadier, or rattail fish, lives in the deep sea. It has a big head and a thin body and tail. The gulper eel's mouth

The black swallower has a huge, stretchy stomach as well as a big mouth. This allows it to digest very large prey.

Amazing!

looks far too big for its long thin body. It opens its huge jaws very wide and scoops up prey twice its own size.

Another big-jawed hunter is the black sea devil, which has lots of long sharp teeth. The sea devil is only seven centimetres long, but it can swallow fish three times its size!

WATCH OUT!

Deep-sea trawling may be harming many deep-sea fish. **Trawlers** drag large heavy nets along the sea floor which catch everything in their path. Apart from fish, the nets catch many other creatures by accident.

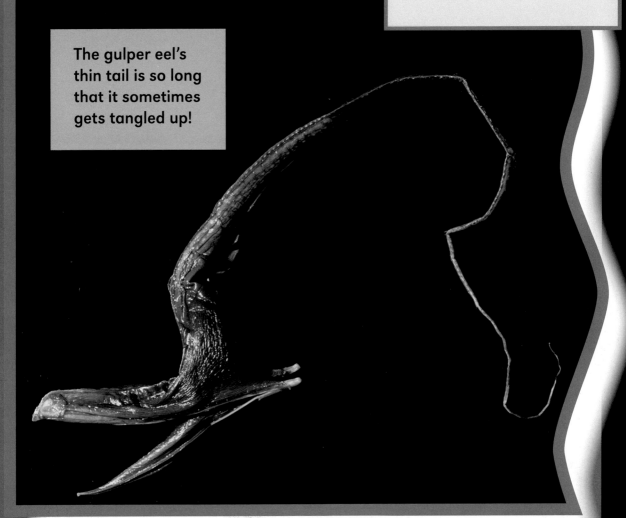

The gulper eel's thin tail is so long that it sometimes gets tangled up!

Light in the darkness

In the darkness of the deep sea, some creatures make their own light. They have special body parts that can produce light.

Lanternfish, dragonfish and hatchetfish have lights along their bellies or sides. The lights make the outline of the fish's body hard to see so they confuse predators. These fish may also use their lights to attract **mates**.

The viperfish uses light to help it catch prey. It has a very long ray on its back fin, which is tipped with a little flap. This flap makes light and shines in the darkness.

Amazing!

The lanternfish can make its lights bright or dim, depending on its surroundings.

Other fish are tempted to have a closer look at the flap, in case it is something tasty to eat, and the sharp-toothed viperfish snaps them up.

The viperfish looks very fierce, but it is only about 30 centimetres long.

Seabed animals

Some deep-sea creatures don't waste energy swimming around to find prey. They wait for prey to come to them. Sea lilies look like plants, but they are really animals. They stay in one place and catch bits of food that drift by with their long feathery arms.

Sea cucumbers live on the floor of the deep sea. These animals are shaped like tubes. They are related to starfish and feed on scraps they find as they crawl around the seabed.

This deep-sea cucumber lives more than 2,000 metres under the sea.

Amazing!

The Japanese giant spider crab lives on the seabed in deep water and is the biggest crab in the world. Its long legs span an incredible four metres – that's more than two very tall humans lying head to toe.

A sea lily can grow new feathery arms if one of them is damaged.

The deep-sea lizardfish also likes to stay close to the sea floor, but it can quickly grab prey in its jaws.

Tripod fish can swim, but they spend much of their time standing on the sea floor on long stiff fins. A tripod fish has special fins behind its head to help it sense anything drifting nearby that it might catch.

Guess what?

Did you know that sponges are animals? Glass sponges live on the floor of the deep sea and feed by **filtering** tiny creatures from the water. They are called glass sponges because the spiky skeleton is made of the same material as glass.

Dark water

Below 1,000 metres the sea is completely dark and very cold – close to freezing. The weight of all the water above creates huge **pressure** which most creatures cannot **survive**. Imagine trying to breathe with lots of elephants sitting on top of you and you will get the idea.

Deep-sea creatures are used to the high pressure and most of them die if they are brought to the surface. One of the many strange creatures that lives in the deep sea is the dumbo octopus. Its name comes from its large fins which look rather like the ears of Dumbo, the elephant in the Disney film. The octopus moves by flapping these fins like wings.

The Dumbo octopus feeds on worms and shellfish that it swallows whole.

The deep-sea fangtooth fish has the biggest teeth for its body size of any animal. They're so big, it cannot close its mouth.

Amazing!

WATCH OUT!

Scientists have discovered that **pollution** from waste dumped in the sea is reaching the deepest depths. They have found **chemicals** in the bodies of deep-sea squid and other creatures.

Sperm whales

Sperm whales dive deeper than any other whales. They often dive down more than 2,000 metres and stay there for over an hour, hunting prey such as squid. A sperm whale eats nearly a ton of food every day.

Sperm whales can grow to 18 metres long – that's longer than three family cars. Each whale has a huge head which is full of an oily liquid called spermaceti. This liquid becomes hard and waxy when it is cold.

The sperm whale has a square-shaped head that can be six metres long.

No one knows exactly why sperm whales have the liquid in their heads, but scientists think it may help them make deep dives and come back to the surface again.

A full-grown male sperm whale weighs 40 tonnes or more – that's more than six elephants.

WATCH OUT!

Fishermen used to hunt sperm whales for their spermaceti, which they used as oil and to make candles, soap and other products. Fewer sperm whales are now killed by hunters, but they can get caught in fishing lines and deep-sea cables. Ocean pollution also harms them.

Amazing!

The sperm whale has the largest brain of any animal.

Deep-sea giants

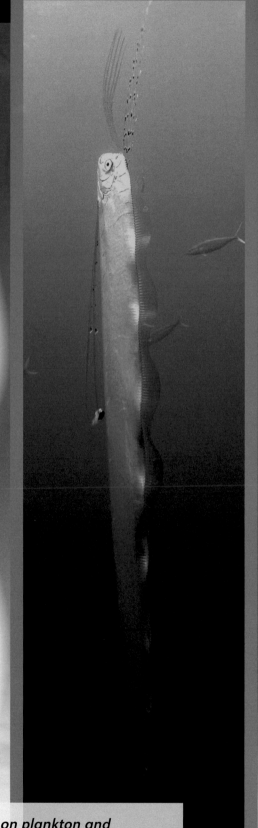

There have always been stories about giant sea monsters such as serpents and dragons. There may not be dragons in the deep sea, but there are some huge and extraordinary creatures.

One of the longest of all fish is the oarfish. Its body is shaped like a ribbon and can grow to ten metres long – almost as long as a bus. It has a long red fin on its back.

Another deep-sea monster is the giant squid, which can grow to be 12 metres long. Giant squid have hardly ever been seen alive, but dead squid have been found in the stomachs of sperm whales.

The huge oarfish feeds on plankton and other small creatures that it strains from the water. It does not appear to have any teeth.

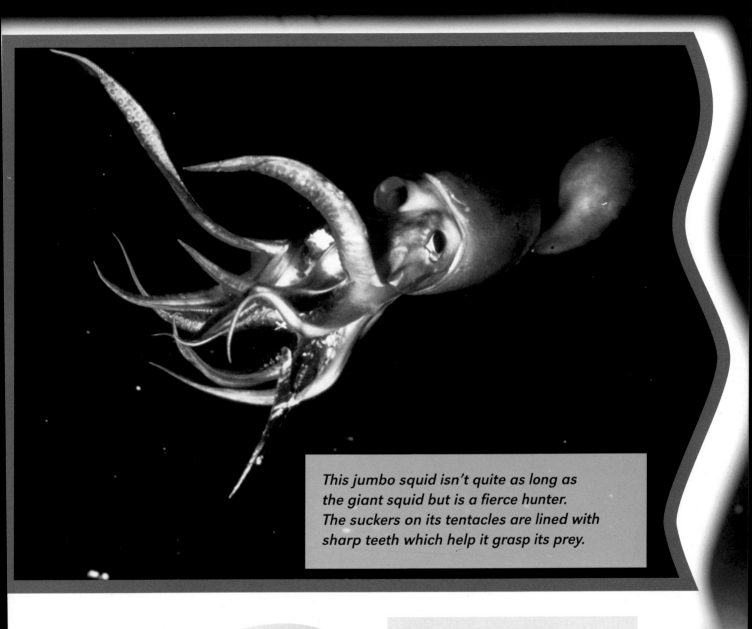

This jumbo squid isn't quite as long as the giant squid but is a fierce hunter. The suckers on its tentacles are lined with sharp teeth which help it grasp its prey.

Amazing!

A giant squid has the largest eyes of any animal. They are 30 centimetres across – bigger than a dinner plate.

Guess what?

Sperm whales and giant squid probably have fierce battles when the whales are hunting the squid. Most sperm whales have scars made by the powerful **suckers** on the giant squid's long **tentacles**.

Bone-eating worms

What do you think happens when a whale dies? Its body slowly sinks to the bottom of the sea. There many different kinds of creatures feast on its huge body.

A female bone-eating worm is about the size of a human finger.

Amazing!

Male bone-eating worms are much smaller than females. The tiny males live attached to females.

Fish, crabs and other animals feed on the dead whale's flesh until only the bones are left. Even these are food for some animals.

Worms called bone-eating snot-flower worms gather on the whale's skeleton. The worms bore into the bones to feed on the fat and oils inside.

The hagfish eats worms and other creatures which it finds by burrowing into the seabed.

Guess what?

Hagfish also eat dead creatures such as whales. The hagfish doesn't have proper jaws. It bores into flesh with its toothed tongue and eats it away.

Finding a mate

Finding a mate in the vast deep sea isn't easy and so some fish don't let go when they do find a partner.

The male anglerfish is tiny compared with the female. He has patches on his head that help him track females by their smell. When he finds one, he attaches himself to her belly and stays there. He takes food from the female's blood. In return, he **fertilizes** her eggs.

Can you see the two little males attached to the back of this female anglerfish?

The hairy angler is a very strange-looking fish. Its body is covered with long spines and hairs that help it pick up the slightest movement in the water.

Amazing!

The football fish is a type of anglerfish with a body that is almost round, like a ball. Male football fish, like other anglerfish, are much smaller than females.

WATCH OUT!
People used to think that waste dumped in the sea would sink to the bottom and stay there. Now we know that sea currents bring some of the waste to the surface again.

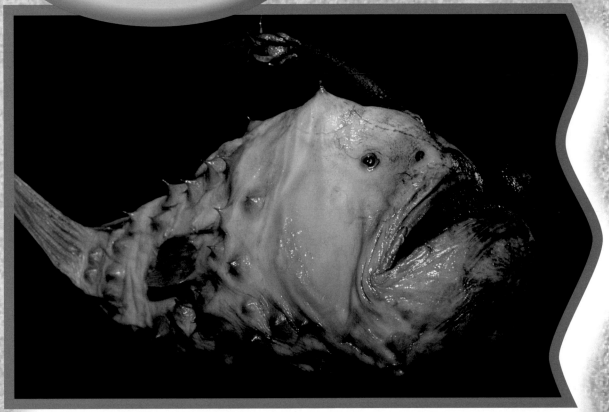

Deep-sea sharks

Sharks are fierce ocean hunters and some of them live in the deep sea. Many of these sharks spend the day in the dark depths. At night they swim up to nearer the surface of the water where they feed.

The cookie-cutter shark gets its name from the way it attacks its prey. This shark latches on to a fish with its suckerlike jaws and digs in with its teeth. Then the shark spins its body round to

The cookie-cutter shark is only about 50 centimetres long, but it attacks much larger animals.

The huge megamouth shark is as long as a small car. This giant feeds mostly on tiny shrimplike creatures and small fish that it filters from the water.

Amazing!

cut out a circle of flesh. Another deep-sea shark is the frill shark, which can grow to be two metres long. Its large mouth is filled with as many as 300 three-pronged teeth – ideal for trapping prey.

WATCH OUT!
The goblin shark is one of the strangest looking sharks. It has a long snout with toothy jaws sticking out beneath and its flabby body is pale pink!

Springs under the sea

In some places, huge springs of water gush out from the sea floor. This water is extremely hot and full of **minerals**. Most creatures cannot survive here, but scientists have discovered plenty of life around these deep-sea vents.

Bacteria live on the minerals in the water and other creatures feed on these bacteria. These include huge tube worms, which can grow to two metres long.

These giant tube worms live beside a deep-sea vent.

WATCH OUT!

Deep-sea vents don't last for ever. Most probably gush for about 30 years before the water stops pouring out. Then the animals must move to another vent or die.

Amazing!

Giant vent mussels grow up to 30 centimetres long – that's three times the size of ordinary mussels.

Vent crabs are some of the fiercest predators around deep-sea vents. They feed on bacteria and also nibble on tube worms.

Pompeii worms also live near vents. They can stand hotter temperatures than any other animal. There are also special kinds of bacteria-eating mussels and clams, as well as crabs that feed on other vent creatures.

A deep-sea fish swims among tube worms.

World oceans: Pacific

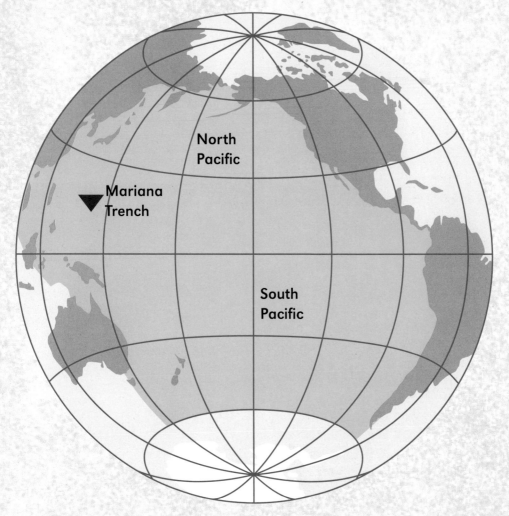

North
Pacific

Mariana
Trench

South
Pacific

The Pacific is the world's largest ocean.
It covers about a third of the surface of the
Earth and is nearly as big as all the land put
together. The Pacific stretches from the Arctic
in the north to the Southern Ocean in the south
and it is bordered by the Americas and by Asia
and Australia. The ocean includes seas such as
the South China Sea and the Tasman Sea.

*The Pacific
Ocean covers
an area about
15 times larger
than the United
States.*

Pacific facts

The deepest point in the Pacific is the Mariana Trench. This is about 11,000 metres deep – that's so deep that it could hold Mount Everest, the world's highest mountain, with room to spare.

The average depth of the Pacific Ocean is just over 4,000 metres.

The Pacific is widest between Indonesia and the coasts of Colombia and Peru, a distance of about 19,800 kilometres.

There are at least 25,000 islands in the Pacific, more than in any other ocean.

The name Pacific comes from the the ocean explorer Ferdinand Magellan (c1480-1521). He called the ocean *Tepre Pacificum*, which means peaceful sea.

The *Victoria* was one of five ships in Ferdinand Magellan's expedition to sail around the world. It was the only ship that completed the journey.

Watery words

bacterium (plural **bacteria**)
A very tiny living thing.

chemicals
Substances that are found in nature or made in a science laboratory. Some chemicals are dangerous and can harm living things.

digest
To break down food so that it can be used by the body.

fertilize
To bring eggs and male sperm together to make young.

filter
To strain from water.

luminous
Something that is luminous makes its own light and shines in the dark.

mate
Male and female animals pair up, or mate, to produce young. An animal's partner is its mate.

minerals
A substance such as calcium or zinc found in nature.

pollution
Things that dirty or damage the natural world, such as litter and oil.

predator
An animal that hunts and kills other animals to eat.

pressure
A force produced by pushing on something. In the deep sea the weight of the water above produces pressure.

prey
An animal hunted and eaten by another animal.

suckers
Cup-shaped parts some animals use to cling to objects.

sunlit zone
The top 200 metres of the ocean which is lit by the sun.

survive
To stay alive.

tentacles
Long body parts that some animals use for feeling and grasping food.

transparent
If something is transparent you can see through it.

trawler
A kind of boat used for fishing.

twilight zone
The twilight zone is between about 200 metres and 1,000 metres below the surface of the sea. There is a little light here, but the further down you go the darker it gets.

Index